Weight Loss for Christians:

Extraordinarily Simple Way

to Conquer Cravings

by Sherry Elaine Evans

PEVEY LEARNING SERVICES PUBLISHING

2012

Published in the United States by Pevey Learning Services Publishing, Spring, TX

Scripture, unless otherwise noted, taken from the Holy Bible, New International Version®, NIV® Copyright 1973, 1978, 1984 by Biblica, Inc.

The "NIV" and "New International Version" are trademarks registered in the United States Patent and Trademark Offices by Biblica, Inc.

Book design by Pevey Learning Services Publishing

Cataloging-in-Publication Data

Evans, Sherry Elaine

> Weight Loss for Christians: Extraordinarily Simple Way to Conquer Cravings

> 61 p.

> Summary: How to rely on specific scripture meditation to help control false food cravings.Written to encourage the Christian struggling with weight issues due to food cravings or food addiction.

> ISBN: 978-0615835334 (pbk.)

Contents

1. My Unanswered Weight Loss Prayer.........7

2. Interpreting Cravings:

   Physical vs. Emotional/Spiritual..............15

3. The Extraordinary Weight Loss Tip.........23

4. Prayer and Meditation.........................31

5. What is Biblical Meditation?......................39

6. The Verses.......................................43

7. Curious About My Diet?............................54

8. Launching Further.............................58

   About the Author..............................60

Disclaimer: The author is not a medical doctor and this book should not be considered to be medical advice. It is always highly recommended that you consult with your medical physician before starting any new diet or weight loss plan.

Dedication:
This book is dedicated to my mother, Caroll, who always believed in the willingness of God to meet our needs. Thank you for passing on the legacy of living while trusting Him.

Other Works by Sherry Elaine Evans:

14 Days of Words with Jesus: How Do I Discover God's Will for Me?

14 Days of Parables with Jesus: Why Is There So Much Trouble in Life?

14 Days of Miracles with Jesus: How Do I See God Working Today?

1.

My Unanswered Prayer

Jesus looked at them and said, "With man this is impossible, but with God <u>all things</u> are possible."
Matthew 19:29

God's truth is <u>truth</u>. The Bible says with God; all things are possible. Yes, that includes your weight loss. You may think that your weight loss issues are not important to God. You may think that your weight goals are impossible to reach.

Why is it easy to believe that God cares about the terminally ill child or the woman battling cancer; but He doesn't care about your weight loss desires?

He does care! The Bible tells us that God knows you well enough to know the number of hairs on your head and to know the thoughts in your heart.

God knows your weight loss goals; and those goals are possible with God's help too.

But how?

For me, I learned the answer to this question through unanswered prayers.

My weight problem story is quite typical. I started gaining excess weight in my early thirties. As a new mother, I packed on pounds that did not easily fall off after my second child was born. Each year, two to five more pounds of fat would plump up and cling on to my thighs and belly. The fat and weight accumulated each and every year for six years. I became more and more out of shape; and more and more tired; and more and more depressed about my weight gain and my lack of energy. Because I was stressed out and tired at the end of the day, I would sit down on the sofa with a magazine or with my laptop to browse internet stories and news. At these times, I always had a snack in hand. Of course, the snack was not celery or carrots or apple sticks. This evening and night time ritual became a regular routine I fell into. It was my "me" time. I'm generally a quiet and introspective personality, and I needed to enjoy some time for myself late at night after the children and their father were in bed. I enjoyed reading and enjoyed snacking; so doing both together made me feel more satisfied, temporarily, at the end of a long day.

Do I have to tell you what happened next? Of course not. You know the consequences I experienced. Since you are reading this book, you may be experiencing similar consequences yourself right now. If you are over the age of 29 and don't exercise regularly, you will gain weight over time. If you are over 29 and you also snack on an extra 600 calories nearly every night before going to bed; then you will gain a lot of weight over time! It's a guaranteed cause and effect equation. I knew what I was doing to myself, but for whatever reason, I was not able to change the cycle. I always believed that whatever weight I put on, I could take off once I decided to "get serious" about my health. My plan was to enjoy myself now; and deal with the excess weight later.

Finally, when I reached the point where I was 40 pounds overweight, and I only had two pairs of pants I could wear (pants that I had originally purchased for when I was about 5 to 6 months pregnant!); I then decided it was time to get serious about my weight loss efforts. However, the decision to get serious about my health and weight loss is exactly the point where my real frustrations began. My original plan -- to enjoy food and snacking first for awhile, and then lose the weight later -- backfired, to say the least.

First, because I was determined to succeed now, I decided to take serious action. We already had a family gym membership that my husband used; so I set up an appointment to get started at the gym. I went to the gym regularly for about a month (one that offered childcare while I worked out!) and I also did additional exercises at home. I read the South Beach Diet® book (which had been published just a year or so before), and I began that diet. But after the first few weeks; I faltered and quit! I couldn't stick with it! My motivation was like a roller coaster ride! My cravings were too powerful! I would still "sneak in" a snack or two into my program I had set up for myself. I would still feel tired and lacking energy at times during the day, so I would reach for a cookie to give me a boost.

Even with some minor cheating on the diet, I did lose about 7 pounds in the first 3 weeks or so; yeah! I was quite happy with this because 7 pounds was almost 20% of my first goal! But then I got distracted and within 2 months of losing those 7 pounds, I had gained them back, plus an additional 7 pounds. I'm not kidding. I lost 7 pounds and then almost immediately gained 14 pounds. I was shocked when standing on the bathroom scale. I actually convinced myself the scale was broken, and I went to the pharmacy near my home and bought a new scale! Sure enough, the brand new scale confirmed the horrible truth. I had gained all the weight back and then doubled it.

My efforts had more than failed. My efforts actually set me back in double the measure! I was frustrated and mad. I was not even sure what had happened. I think what happened was I changed my diet so much that my metabolism slowed. Then when I entered the next phase of the diet where I was allowed to eat more, I gained all the weight back and then doubled it.

Needless to say, I was ready to give up. Now I had no pants that fit. I refused to go out and buy bigger pants, so I just used some elastic and a safety pin to expand the waist of the two pairs of pants I could still squeeze into; and I continued to wear those two pairs of pants. That was very depressing to me.

Finally, I began to pray about my weight

loss with more focus. When I prayed,

the unexpected happened.

Nothing!

That's right, nothing happened. God didn't do anything to help me! *Or at least that is what it seemed*, and that is what I thought at first. In retrospect, I see that this unanswered prayer was necessary for me to learn what the root of my weight problem really was. **My weight problem was not due to lack of faith.** I had strong faith God could fix me and help me. **No, my weight problems were due to my priorities in my life, my thought patterns, and the way I poorly handled stress in my life. Nearly every day, I had been turning to food to soothe me, instead of turning to the word of God -- which would have soothed my soul better than the richest of foods and desserts.**

I really do wish I could write that I prayed and God helped me through the prayer alone. I wish I could share with you some of the effective prayers I prayed that immediately supercharged my metabolism and melted off the pounds! I wish it had been that simple. But the truth is that I prayed and prayed but God did not seem to respond. Even with prayer, I completely stumbled, and I was not able to demonstrate self-control in my habits. I just could not break free from my own poor eating choices and poor health habits.

Now let me be clear. I did not just pray for a day or two. I had prayed to God for help with losing weight for nearly a year. I was frustrated and thought that God did not care.

God is all powerful, right?

And my request would be so simple for Him, correct?

Forty pounds of my human fat is not too big a job for God, right?

God could have easily granted my prayer by zapping me with a renewed motivation, right?

My body is His temple, right?

So why wasn't He helping me?

After all, God created me; and I knew it was in His will for me to take the best care of my body. I felt like I was asking a very simple and very doable prayer. I had seen miracles of God in my family much bigger than this request. I felt frustrated with God and frustrated with myself. I became convinced that maybe losing weight shouldn't be such a big priority for me after all. Maybe I was being selfish in my request. I began to feel dumb for even asking God to help.

As I close this introductory chapter, I do hope that I have not offended you in any way by focusing on how God, in the beginning, did not help me through my prayers. I am definitely not negating the power of prayer. Not by any means! Please don't misunderstand me, I <u>certainly</u> believe in the power of prayer. I share my story above with you, because I believe the steps and thoughts and doubts I went through in my prayer life are the same steps many Christians go through when a prayer seems to be unanswered.

I tell my story because you can probably relate to many parts of it. In my case, the unanswered prayers eventually led me to a new understanding of the difference between my physical needs and my spiritual needs. I also learned the value and the power of biblical meditation. Biblical meditation became a new priority in my life; and it became the new habit I developed which turned my struggle around.

2.

Interpreting Cravings:
Physical vs. Emotional/Spiritual

In this chapter, I am going to help you to see that God has already given you an extraordinary mechanism which will guide you in getting to your best weight for your health - and this mechanism works to rid yourself of excess weight and internal toxins faster than you thought possible.

What most of us do not understand is that we have both physical cravings (for food) and we have spiritual cravings (for time with the Lord). Quite simply, we usually confuse the two types of cravings; thinking that both types of cravings are for food. Once you understand that your food cravings sometimes are for food and sometimes are for emotional/spiritual things; then you simply need to learn to be able to tell the difference. Then you will feed your true food cravings with physical food. And you will feed your false food cravings with spiritual food.

Physical Hunger vs. Emotional/Spiritual Hunger and Thoughts on 'Bestselling' Diet Plans

Throughout the Bible, both in the Old Testament and the New Testament; there are comparisons and contrasts made between physical hunger and spiritual hunger. I do think that in today's time, when we are busy and preoccupied and most of us don't actually spend regular time focusing on the Lord; that **we are mixing up our physical hunger with what may very well be a spiritual hunger.** As an example, look at the very words of Jesus when he was enduring temptation in the desert - specifically he was enduring temptation to eat when he was purposefully fasting:

"It is written: 'Man does not live on bread alone, but by every word that comes from the mouth of God.'" - Matthew 4:4

Could it be any more clear that we have both a true physical need for food and a true spiritual need for knowing and spending time in the word of God? Jesus himself overcame the temptation to turn stones to bread and eat by using an intentional recitation, or a meditation, of scripture.

Because the weight loss method I recommend for Christians is psychologically based on monitoring your cravings; I don't specifically endorse or recommend any particular diet plan. **I write this book because I don't believe that any of the available bestselling diet books or diet programs address how to handle and overcome cravings effectively. The reason we don't lose weight is because we cannot handle our cravings and we therefore do not have self-control in following a plan.** Anyone who has tried to stick to a diet and failed knows that the main reason they fail is because they cannot control their appetite or their cravings!

This is why year after year after year, a new #1 bestselling diet book is published. If the diets were truly effective, then there wouldn't be a new bestselling diet plan each year, right? **This is because the problem with being overweight really has nothing to do with the overweight person needing a new diet plan.** The problem for the vast majority of overweight people is that they cannot control their appetite or their cravings. Isn't this obvious? To me, this is common sense! Where are the diet books that teach you to control your cravings and impulses? Do any others exist? I'm sure there are some out there, but I have yet to see many. Perhaps they don't exist because the secular world does not realize that, much of the time, the false food cravings are actually spiritual cravings for a level of satisfaction that physical food can never provide.

The most popular, mass-marketed, bestselling diet plans generally don't even address how to manage food cravings. Most of the time, the recommendation is for the dieter to suffer through cravings for a week or two, and eventually the cravings will go away. Have you tried to do that? - I have! I have suffered through a week or two of cravings; hoping and believing that they would just magically disappear after that time frame - and guess what? They don't! **Your cravings will never go away until you fill them with what they really want and what you really need! You want and you need 'living food' and 'living water!' It is spiritual food and wisdom you crave.** This is what I truly know and believe! Of course, because most diet books are written for the secular market; the majority of them certainly do not write from the perspective that unnecessary food cravings likely represent an emotional or spiritual longing that is begging to be filled.

The void can be filled instead, and more effectively, by relying on the word of God.

Yes, that is a bold statement. In fact, I know that I will be ridiculed by critics for making such a statement and taking the perspective that I do on weight management. However, let's use common sense and let's think about this together:

What is an unnecessary food craving? It is a craving for something to satisfy you in some way. If you have just recently eaten, at least within the past three hours, you know your body does not need more food or food treats. You are falsely interpreting these unnecessary food cravings. The cravings give you a signal, and you interpret that signal as a need or desire for more food or treats. However, your unnecessary cravings are actually a signal to you that you need to satisfy one of two things:

1) your emotions or

2) your human nature to seek temporary pleasure.

When you have an unnecessary craving, the signal is actually telling you that you need to do something to satisfy either your emotions or your need for pleasure. Food does satisfy this need, but temporarily -- only for an hour or two. If you choose to satisfy thosee 'false' craving signals with meditation or focus on the Lord; the true source of those cravings will be fully satisfied. Read the truth of this in the verses from Isaiah below:

> *Why spend money on what is not bread, and your labor on what does not satisfy? Listen, listen to me, and eat what is good, and your soul will delight in the richest of fare. - Isaiah 55:2*

I believe this verse in Isaiah tells us to listen to the words of the Lord; to allow the Lord to be our delight; and not to fill ourselves with substitutes that do not satisfy the soul. We are told to "listen...and eat what is good." These verses are poetic of course, and not literal. We are being encouraged to feed our unnecessary cravings with worship, study, and meditation on God's word! Then, and only then, will the source of such cravings truly be satisfied. Not only will they be satisfied; but they will also be satisfied even more than if we had just indulged in the "richest of fare!"

I also like the modern paraphrase of this passage in Isaiah from "The Message," which writes the verses into our modern "street language":

Why do you spend your money on junk food, your hard-earned cash on cotton candy? Listen to me, listen well: Eat only the best, fill yourself with only the finest. Pay attention, come close now, listen carefully to my life-giving, life-nourishing words.

-Isaiah 55:2 from The Message

We will find our best and finest nourishment in the life-giving, life-nourishing words of the Lord! Daily closeness with Him is what we are truly craving - not junk food, not candy, not excessively large meals! This principle of a spiritual hunger needing to be filled is also emphasized again in the Beatitudes in the New Testament:

Blessed are those who hunger and thirst for righteousness, for they will be filled. - Matthew 5:6

Because I use daily meditations and "mini-devotionals" to overcome my cravings; the cravings do not control me. Therefore, because I am not controlled by my cravings, I also do not have to follow a strict diet plan. **When the cravings don't control you, you can generally eat what you want and stay in moderation without much extra effort.** This is why I am not recommending a particular diet or eating plan. Instead, I recommend a spiritual plan!

3.

The Extraordinary Weight Loss Tip

I do have one practical, significant tip that helps me immensely; and I am going to share it with you now. I share this because I know this tip will likely help you too. I call this the 'extraordinary weight loss tip', and it is explained below:

__Extraordinary Weight Loss Tip__: Interpret all of your cravings to determine if they are true hunger signals or not! __A true craving is a physical signal that comes from the stomach.__ Determine if your craving signal is coming from your stomach or not. Then, eat only *when your craving indicates a true hunger signal. If it is not a true hunger signal, use a meditation, or time otherwise spent with focus on the Lord, to satisfy what is most likely the true source of the craving.*

I call this 'the extraordinary weight loss tip' because these signals are an extraordinary design mechanism from God. God gave us the ability to tell the difference between true hunger and emotional/spiritual hunger. If you combine Biblical meditation with the 'extraordinary weight loss tip'; you will lose the weight fast; and you will keep it off for good. Losing a half-pound or more each day in the first ten days is not uncommon.

Here is how the extraordinary weight loss tip works for me. When I feel a craving start to overcome me, I make every effort to pause and try to determine if the desire I am having is a signal of true hunger; or if it is just a craving for some other type of satisfaction. I do this by actually thinking and focusing on the condition of my stomach at the time the craving occurs. I ask myself, "Is my stomach telling me it is empty or almost empty?" **If your stomach is near empty, then you should experience a tightening feeling, or a "pulling feeling" coming from the inside of the stomach. Then you know it is a true hunger signal.** Of course, if your stomach is actually growling loudly, that is very likely a signal that it is true hunger for physical food!

 A true hunger signal from the stomach is different than an unnecessary craving begging to be satisfied. Typically, you will feel an unnecessary craving in your head, face, or mouth; but not in your stomach. It may be a slight headache; or a tickling feeling near your forehead. Also, if you have been presented with a food or treat and you are not truly hungry; the craving may take place by noticing increased salivation in your mouth. Sometimes I feel the unnecessary craving in my thoughts! I will 'hear' my own thoughts say to myself, "I just want it! I want it, and I can have it just because it is in front of me and I want it! I can always eat less or exercise more....tomorrow!" When you have these types of symptoms, they are not symptoms of true hunger; and you should not feed these unnecessary cravings with food. Instead, when I experience those types of false cravings, I now overcome them with Biblical meditations or with time spent focused on the Lord or His word. Often times the verses I rely on during these times of temptation are very short:

"Taste and see that the Lord is good!;" or

"Isn't life more than food?"

You should feed false cravings with meditations or time with God; and you should feed true, stomach-based hunger cravings with food. This means that if you are not having a true stomach-based hunger signal,then you do not eat. You should eat your meals and snacks when you have a true hunger signal from your stomach; and not eat at other times. *The only exception to this is in the morning for breakfast.* Research does show that having breakfast helps greatly with any weight loss plan; so what I recommend is this: if you wake up in the morning, and you do not have a true stomach-based hunger signal; go ahead and eat something light that is about 100 to 150 calories (a cup of light yogurt and ½ apple or pear, for example.) Then wait for your next true, stomach-based hunger signal before you eat again for a snack or for lunch.

Now, I will admit that there is a social difficulty that comes with this extraordinary weight loss strategy, so you have to figure out how to handle various situations that may arise. For example, what do you do if your family eats at regular times or if you have a regular lunch time at work? What if it is "time to eat" a meal with others; and you don't have a true hunger signal, and you still want to participate in the meal for the social aspect of it? You will have to figure out how you will respond in these situations.

Here is how I handle these situations -- I keep enough food supplies on hand to be able to throw together a light salad with vegetables and a low calorie dressing; or I have a cup of vegetable soup that is 60 calories or below for the entire cup of soup (Progresso® brand has some good ones at the supermarket). I eat the salad or soup with my family or co-workers; and then save my actual lunch or dinner portions to eat when I am actually hungry. I suppose I could sit with my friends or family and not eat; but for some reason, my not eating often seems to make the others at the table uncomfortable. So that is why I have the salad or low calorie soup for those times. You don't necessarily have to eat a very light salad or soup at these times. You could have any small snack, under 100 calories or so, at those times. If the meal is a shared meal, like at family dinner time, of course you can easily just eat a few bites with your family, then set the plate aside and heat it up in the microwave later when you do have a true stomach-based hunger signal.

So to summarize the extraordinary weight loss tip simply: If your stomach isn't giving you a clear signal that it is near empty and needs to be filled, then don't eat unless:

1) it is breakfast time shortly after you have woken up. If this is the case, eat something about 100 to 150 calories to start up your metabolism for the day.

or

2)   it is a social eating time when you are expected to eat. At these times, eat a very low calorie salad, soup, or other snack and then eat your true meal alone, later when you have a true hunger signal. Or if it is a shared meal like at family dinner time, just eat a few bites slowly with your family, and save the rest to be re-heated so you may enjoy it later in the day or evening when you do have a true hunger signal.

Next, if your stomach is <u>not</u> telling you it is truly hungry, and <u>instead you get a craving signal coming from another part of your body</u> (usually the head, face, or mouth area); then <u>use those cravings as opportunities to meditate, pray, or read the Bible or spend time with God in other ways, such as reading a good bible study book or listening to or singing a song of worship.</u> You will squash those false signals away with scripture verses; and at the same time you will feed your spiritual needs as you draw ever closer to the Lord, your Creator.

The best part of the extraordinary tip is that you are equipping yourself with an internal signal to spend time with God! Isn't it a wonderful gift to have a signal like that? It's better than an alarm clock or a pre-programmed wake-up call. It is a biological reminder, and you never have to remember to reset the signal. It will always work as a reminder to you, so that you can continually return to God's word and to an awareness of His presence throughout the day.

Delight yourself in the LORD and he will give you the desires of your heart. - Psalms 37:4

Now finally, there is one more aspect, or general guideline to follow, with this extraordinary weight loss tip. **When you have a true hunger signal and you begin eating to satisfy your stomach; continue to monitor that hunger signal as you eat; and when the signal turns off or dissipates - then stop eating!** This was a big "ah-hah" for me. It meant that if my stomach felt better after eating only ½ of what was on my plate; then I stopped eating. It meant that if I was having a granola bar or a cup of yogurt for a snack; then I didn't have to eat the whole thing. Yes, this meant that there were often half-eaten granola bars in my kitchen in plastic baggies, waiting for a true hunger signal before they were consumed! But it works, this strategy works!

If you are reading this for the first time, you may think that stopping mid-snack or mid-meal is going to be very difficult for you. However, if you do the two following things:

1) Meditate on scripture (or pray or read the Bible) to banish false cravings and instead feed your true spiritual needs;

and

2) Rely on true stomach-based hunger signals to know when to start and when to stop eating your snacks and meals;

Then you will then find that those two lifestyle behaviors will be much easier to implement successfully when you do them together; rather than trying to implement one or the other alone.

4.

Prayer and Meditation

I do believe in the power of prayer. *I also believe in the power of the lessons that can be learned from unanswered prayer.* In this chapter, I want to return to my personal story, and consider some reasons as to why my initial prayers alone were not answered in the way I had hoped.

God often does not answer prayer in the way we expect. The important lesson overall here is this: **When God doesn't answer in the way we expect or hope for; it is because He knows a better way. He has a better plan; or He has something for us to learn about Him. He has to deny our direct request so that we are not misled. He has to deny our direct request so that we may find His methods and His ways.**

"For my thoughts are not your thoughts, and neither are your ways, my ways, declares the Lord."

-Isaiah 55:8

Eventually I came to understand that **God did not answer my prayer, at first, because he wanted me to discover something that may be even more powerful than prayer alone. God wanted me to learn to use the power available through reading and meditating on His Word. God wanted me to replace my bad habits with habits that would help me to focus and rely more deeply on Him and His word.**

Before I recognized that I needed spiritual food instead of physical food, I realized that I was addicted to snacking and overeating. I was an addict! I was bound in a vicious, destructive cycle. Just as an alcoholic is addicted to alcohol, I was addicted to satiating my cravings with snacks. Just as excess alcohol will ruin the life of the person who imbibes; my poor food choices were slowing ruining my life, stealing my energy, and stealing my joy during a time of my life when I should have been enjoying some of the best years of my life with my family.

My nightly snacking and reading rituals were not just simple, harmless "me"time. I was caught in a cycle of addiction. In order to handle this addiction, I had to overcome it in God's way -- by using the powerful word of the Lord as my conquering weapon!

I meditate on your precepts and consider your ways.

I delight in your decrees; I will not neglect your word.
-Psalms 119:15-16

Just praying to God and simply waiting on Him to act was not enough. **God wants us to draw close to Him;** and **then** he guides us. The Bible says, "Draw near to

God; and then He will draw near to you." (James 4:8) Yes, we can draw near to God through prayer. Many Christians do get closer to God through prayer. **The truth for me, however, was that I was not using prayer to be close to God. My heart was not in the right place. I was not seeking Him first. I was using prayer mostly to thank Him and then to make requests of Him.** When I began reading the Bible more and meditating on certain verses which helped me understand the right priorities for my life; then I actually truly began to draw nearer to God.

And when I focused on drawing nearer to Him, He then met my needs and requests in full. I sought His truth first, and then the rest of my needs were met. (Matthew 6:33) The actions I needed to take became clearer. When I chose to focus on God's word, I finally gained a truly supernatural motivation which literally conquered my cravings.

Many well known Bible teachers teach about the need to meditate on God's word. Beth Moore of *Living Proof Ministries* comes to my mind as one of my favorites. The power of meditation is discussed in *The Purpose Driven Life* by Rick Warren. I had read and learned some from Christian leaders about meditation. So on some level, I knew that meditating on God's word could be useful. I had even completed a Beth Moore Bible study where she taught us to write verses on cards and meditate on them throughout the day. (I listened to her but I didn't do it at the time, because I really didn't understand what Biblical meditation was, and I really didn't think I had the time for it.) Meditation wasn't really taught in my church, though; and it wasn't something I even considered putting into action.

Eventually though, here is what happened for me to come to an understanding of all of this. During some time spent in Bible reading one day, I came across a verse that just "zapped" me. If you read and study the Bible with some regularity; you know what I am referring to and you understand the experience I am talking about. I can't explain the "zap" experience fully in words here. Some people may say that the scripture just really "spoke to their heart." For me though, it wasn't a soft nudging of the heart. No, nothing gentle like a nudge -- as I said, the verse just zapped me, like a slap to the forehead combined with an "ah ha!" moment! In one moment, within a very short passage, the Lord had given words just for me and for my specific situation. After the years of prayer, he gave me the answer. And here is the irony: I already had the answer in His word. I had actually committed this scripture to memory previously, and I already knew it well . But I had never thought to apply it to my weight and dieting trials.

What was the verse that ended up zapping me, or slapping me, on the forehead in a precise spiritual way? Not ironically, it is one of the few verses in the Bible that refers to both food and emotions in the same sentence!

Therefore I tell you, do not worry about your life, what you will eat or drink; or about your body, what you will wear. Is not life more than food..? - Matthew 6:25

Previously, whenever I had read or considered this verse, I had always place emphasis on the phrase "*Do not worry about....*" However, when I read Matthew 6:25 this time, I read it with an emphasis on the phrase "*Is not life more than food?*" Suddenly, my entire way of thinking about food was transformed in an instant.

Getting spiritually "zapped" from time to time can be a good thing. It can light your motivation on fire. But motivational fires often burn out quick (like at the very next mealtime, perhaps?) This is when review of the scripture and meditation plays an important key role to keeping the motivational fires fanned and burning throughout the rest of the day, throughout the next day and week, and throughout the long journey that is required in changing poor habits.

The word of God can, and does, transform in an instant. And after that instant has passed, the continued reading and focusing on the word of God maintains the transformation. Biblical reading and meditation is the practice that leads to strong and long term maintenance of the transformation.

Through all of this, I learned that when we pray, we should be open to finding the answer to the prayer in God's word. It's okay to hope for a miracle answer to the prayer. God is the master of miracles too, after all. However, it is imperative to also be in God's word, because His word has power; and meditating on his word gives perseverance. Even more importantly, meditating on His word is effective in maintaining long term and permanent change of habits. It can help to usher in what will become a true, long-lasting, and complete transformation.

I have now learned that meditating on God's Word can truly help to overcome all obstacles in my life, weight loss included. For me, the practice of meditation began as part of an effort to help change my weight and to shrink my body size. However my entire weight loss experience and conquering of my appetite story is now much bigger than a mere weight loss success testimonial. Now that I am in better shape I also have more energy to love God more and to serve Him. I also have more energy for the ones I love most in my life, as the mother and wife in my family.

Even more exciting is this: I now have a quite a visible testimony to the power of God's word in my life! As my physical figure improved and continues to improve; I have a new opportunity to share with others about God's word! Without surprise, when friends and others started seeing me, they would ask what I was doing to lose weight! That now allows me to tell about God's word in a profound and personally meaningful way that I have never been able to do before.

My weight loss journey has just been the start, too. Today, the act of meditation has spilled over into many other areas of my life. The act of Biblical meditation has brought me closer to the Lord and has enabled me to love Him more and more. It has enabled me gain more of an understanding of His ways. Now I am a more eager and a more effective minister to others both within my family and beyond.

5.

What is Biblical Meditation?

I do want to take some time to explain Biblical meditation. What is it, exactly?

Biblical meditation is NOT a spiritual practice to attempt to "empty the mind" in order to connect with God or with an alter-consciousness.

Okay, I just wanted to clear that up. It can be a common misunderstanding.

Previously, when I thought of the meaning of the word *meditation*, I did think of spiritual practices such as I've seen or read about in Buddhism. It is important to understand that this is <u>not</u> what I am referring to when I talk about meditation on Bible verses or on the Word.

Let's look at the basic dictionary definitions for the word meditate and meditation:

med·i·tate

1. To reflect on; contemplate.

2. To plan in the mind; intend.

2. In Buddhism or Hinduism - To train, calm, or empty the mind, often by achieving an altered state, as by focusing on a single object.

3. To engage in devotional contemplation, especially prayer.

4. To think or reflect, especially in a calm and deliberate manner.

As you can see, the word meditate, in its most basic definition, simply means to reflect on or to contemplate, especially in a deliberate manner. The definition related to eastern religious practices is an exception, or a specialized use, of the word.

So when a Christian meditates on scripture; it merely means that he or she is deliberately thinking, or reflecting, on the words from God. Biblical meditation is intentionally focusing on the scriptures as the word of God. It is not a New Age type practice. There is no humming. No mantras. No "emptying" of the mind. Biblical meditation is the act of filling your mind with God's truth and allowing it to redirect your thinking and your attitudes. A meditation like this can take just seconds to do. Or it can take longer depending on the situation. Meditation on scripture is encouraged throughout the Bible, and especially in the Psalms and in Proverbs.

Often when I meditate on particular verses, I will also create a mental image, or a visualization in my mind. Again, this is a visual reflection on the scripture and it only lasts for seconds. Many people respond to visuals better than word memory and word meanings. For this reason developing some mental imagery to help you connect the meaning of the verses to your life situation may also be helpful. We can often connect more readily with the significance of a verse by associating it with a visual in our minds.

In the next chapter, as I discuss the specific verses I used in my weight loss meditations; I also give some examples of the visualizations I created. I share my visualizations to help you understand that any visualization used in Biblical meditation is also very simple. Your visualizations don't have to be the same as mine; and you may not want to use visualization at all. It's up to you.

In closing this chapter, I do believe that the Bible clearly demonstrates that God wants us to meditate on his precepts regularly as part of meeting our spiritual needs. We are told "whatever you do; do it all for the glory of God." The Christian's ability to fulfill this command becomes more possible when meditation is used throughout the Christian's day. Whatever you do throughout the day can eventually become a testimony and an act to glorify God! It is my hope that this book will help so many people transform their physical and spiritual lives, not just for their own health, but for the great testimony of the Lord's power that will follow. I want you to have a new, personal testimony of the actual power of God's word and His work in your life! I hope that you learn to transfer your cravings for bad and excess foods to a craving for closeness with the Father. I pray that you will also develop a powerful testimony that will point to the glory of God and to the power of His word!

6.

The Verses

In this section, I share with you the six main Bible verses I meditated on to conquer my cravings and to stop myself before succumbing to the temptation of unnecessary snacking or overindulging.

Here is the specific process I relied on:

1) First, I memorized each verse.

2) In most cases, I also developed specific visual imagery to help me best apply the words of the verses to my specific desires and temptations.

3) Then, in the morning as I prepared for the day, and frequently throughout the day, I would review and reflect on these verses and recall the images I had created in my mind. If a particular fierce sugar craving hit me, for example, I would think on a verse more intentionally, sometimes while closing my eyes and focusing on breathing deeply for a few breaths. I would do this until I could feel the cravings or temptation leave me.

Sometimes, of course, the desire to eat wouldn't completely leave me (we do have a natural, God given hunger drive, after all); but the desire to overindulge would melt away.

I do want to insert here that I was eating regularly every day. In fact, I usually ate between 1400 and 1900 calories every day; and I continue to eat in that range today. I am in no way recommending that you use meditation in order to completely stop eating or to eat so little that you are hurting yourself physically. The minimum calories to eat a day is generally recommended to be 1200. Always consult with your medical physician before starting any significant dieting or health change too, of course.

We have all heard it said that the only path to true, long-term, successful weight loss is lifestyle change. Believe me, adding regular Bible meditation to your life is one of the greatest lifestyle changes you can implement, both for your physical health, your emotional health, and your spiritual health!

I have one question to address before I start listing the verses I used. What do you do if you discover that memorizing and recalling the scriptures, as recommended, is too difficult, or just not effective, for you? If that is the case, then you should write these verses on index cards (or enter them into your smart phone if you use one) and keep them in your wallet or pocket or handbag. You can then review them easily throughout the day. When a particular strong craving or temptation strikes, just pull out the scripture cards or pull up the notes in your smart phone to review them. Eventually, you most likely will memorize the verses and find that bringing them to your mind is a natural response to many of your daily happenings.

Verse 1

***Love the Lord your God with all your heart and with all your soul and with all your strength and with all your mind.* -Luke 10:27**

This verse reminds us that when God is our "all in all;" He is meeting all our needs. Because we rely on Him to meet our needs; we do not have to try to satisfy our physical desires on our own. When we realize that God is, and should be, our primary focus of our cravings; then we are able to demonstrate the utmost in self-control. Our soul craves time with God; even more than our physical bodies crave the foods that we don't even need to be eating in the first place.

Let's face it; most of the time we eat the way we do because we are trying to satisfy our physical selves in some way. If we are already overweight, then there is no true physical need to continue to keep snacking, overindulging, or overeating. We are merely feeding a craving. Meditation on Luke 10:27 helps us to redirect that craving away from foods and flavors; and towards the truth of God's love for us.

This week, when you are tempted by a craving; instead of indulging yourself; repeat this verse and meditate on it. Say, "I want to love the Lord my God with all my heart and with all my soul and with all my strength and with all my mind!" I do not want cookies and crackers to fill me! I want His word and presence and love to fill me!

When you acknowledge that your desire is to be in His will, then you will find your worldly desires dissipate; while your cravings for scripture, for prayer, and even for healthy foods will increase.

Verse 2

"Hast thou found honey? Eat so much as is sufficient for thee, lest thou be filled therewith, and vomit it."

~Proverbs 25:16 (KJV)

Proverbs 15:16 pretty much speaks clearly and provides quite a vivid image in itself, doesn't it? How wise the author of this Proverb was! This verse makes me laugh a bit, because the image I associate with it is quite vivid and even comical. The verse does definitely make me stop and think, especially at those times when an unexpected treat or dessert is offered to me. At first, I would say the verse to myself and visualize myself eating something sweet and sugary, while immediately feeling nauseated and ready to throw it up. Then I would imagine a little caricature of a man belching with his tongue out. This would cause my stomach to churn just enough that I lost the desire for anything more than a taste of the treat. Eventually, I no longer had to put myself through the visualization, and recalling the words alone became effective.

I can't say that reflecting on this verse actually drew me closer to experiencing the love of the Lord. Bringing the proverb to mind, however, helped me immensely during the first few weeks of my 'diet.' It made me appreciate that vast breadth of practical and spiritual wisdom that is in the Bible. I used this verse specifically when I stumbled across an unexpected treat! For example, I used the verse if someone offered me a slice of cake that I knew I shouldn't eat that day. It came to the point that all I would have to say to myself is, "Hast thou found honey?" And I would then laugh to myself and easily pass on the tempting opportunity.

I also realized that today's truth in Proverbs 25:16 is that if I did not stop indulging in sugary and processed foods, that I would eventually end up sick. If I was fortunate enough to avoid a problem like heart disease or diabetes or cancer, I would still experience a milder level of sick involving simply "not feeling good" most of the time; and living with a lack of energy and vitality.

So when you stumble across some unexpected "honey;" or when you are tempted by sweets, or chocolate pie, or by something that only serves to strip you from your good health; just remember this verse; and then take only a little if you must. You can use the proverb to remind yourself that consuming sugar does cause an inflammatory response in your body. Remind yourself that if you eat too much, you may feel emotionally sick and disgusted with yourself for not exhibiting self-control and for "blowing" your healthier lifestyle.

Verse 3

Therefore I tell you, do not worry about your life, what you will eat or drink; or about your body, what you will wear. Is not life more than food..? - Matthew 6:25

Matthew 6:25 is verse that speaks directly to emotions and food! Specifically we are told to not be anxious about what we eat or drink. Likewise, we should not allow ourselves to become anxious or grumpy or bitter over the fact that we know there are things that we should not eat, even as those very items may be right in front of us!

Is life not more than food? We know that seeking God and spiritual growth and relationships with others is what is important, right? Did you skip over that slice of pizza today? That is ok, and you won't miss it! Did you refrain from adding a second lump of sugar to your coffee this morning? Good job! Did you skip over your prayer time or time with God though? Do you wonder why your self control may be slipping? Maybe it has very little to do with "giving in" to your food cravings and bad habits and instead has more to do with skipping time spent with the One who will sustain you through this time of change for you!

During that first week of your diet change; you may start to feel grumpy or anxious or even jittery if you are used to a high caffeine or high sugar or processed foods diet. If you are like I was, you might even feel jealous if your co-worker or friend decides to indulge and have extra slices of pizza when you know you can't have any today. When you feel those emotions start to rise, remind yourself that you will not be anxious about your diet or about food! You know that life is not about that slice of pizza! You know that life is about so much more than the chocolate cake! And if you do start to feel depressed over your dieting requirements and progress; know that the Lord will sustain you through it. Thank Him for that!

Verse 4

"Taste and see that the Lord is Good! Blessed is the one who takes refuge in Him!"-Psalms 34:8

Oh this verse is such a good one for me! I use it very frequently! I use this verse whenever I wander towards the kitchen pantry, looking for a snack mid-day or late at night when I am working or writing while the rest of the family is asleep. I find this verse to be a very effective reminder that time with the Lord will satisfy me so much greater than any snack can! The words of the Lord and the love of the Lord are so much more fulfilling! For this meditation, I actually visualize that I am receiving a hug from Jesus. Yes, I rely on this verse and this visualization very frequently. I find that visualizing the hug really calms me and redirects my thinking away from cravings and towards Him.

Verse 5

For the kingdom of God is not a matter of eating or drinking, but of righteousness, peace, and joy in the Holy Spirit, because anyone who serves Christ in this way is pleasing to God..." Romans 14:17-18

This verse really helps me stay in the right mindset! Yes there are times when I may be tempted to believe that a large bowl of ice cream will bring me the "joy of the kingdom" itself. At least temporarily. Sometimes a slice of key lime pie can appear like a slice of heaven to my tastebuds.

The truth to emphasize in these verse is that the kingdom of heaven is not about eating and drinking! It is about righteousness and peace, and joy in the Holy Spirit! These thoughts take me back to the idea of wanting to love God with my whole heart. I want to be filled with the joy of loving Him. I choose to fill myself with meditations on this verse, bringing me the joy, the peace, and even the cheerful correction that comes from reading His word. Then, because I am filled with focusing on the important things of heaven, I cannot simultaneously be filled with urges and lies to myself that dessert is a manifestation of heaven on earth. It's not.

Again, keep your mind on the things of the Lord; become skilled at simple meditations on his Word, and spending time in His will and in wonder about Him. Then you simply cannot simultaneously keep your mind on human temptations, greeds, and desires.

The final thought I have for the Romans 14 verses is that by associating joy with the Holy Spirit, instead of in food; we are doing what we know is right for our earthly bodies. If you continue to read Romans 14, the scripture also continues on and suggests that being an example in this way "does serve Christ, and is pleasing to Him."

Verse 6

"I will bless the Lord at all times, His praise shall continually be in my mouth." - Psalms 34:1

I think Psalms 34:1 sums it all up nicely, doesn't it? By meditating on God's word regularly, we are keeping his words in our mouth and in our mind. These meditations and time spent with God are so much more fulfilling than any foods we can put in our mouths. For this meditation, it is a bit embarrassing for me to reveal the image I use. But I actually visualize myself sucking on a candy with the words of scripture on it. Then, as I allow the candy to dissolve on my tongue, I also satisfy and bring an end to any craving I may have been experiencing.

7.

Curious About My Diet?

I know that I said in a previous chapter that I do not recommend a specific diet plan. I recommend a spiritual plan focused on managing cravings and interpreting your craving signals. You feed the true cravings with food, and you do not feed the false food cravings with food. It's simple and I believe implementing this in your life is all you really need to get to a healthier weight. However, I have been asked this question so many times, "Well, how did you change your eating habits?" So, I do want to address the question here as well. I am going to share with you generally what kind of diet or eating plan I do follow.

Again, I believe that Biblical meditation along with the extraordinary weight loss tip will be effective even if you don't have a specific diet plan. However, I know you may be curious about what kind of diet I do follow, so here is an outline:

I generally have 1500-1600 calories a day; and usually no more than 500 to 600 calories in one meal or one eating session. My preferred exercise is walking outside for about two miles or doing a 20 to 30 minute aerobics video in my living room. But honestly, I typically only do formal exercise about once a week; even though my goal is to increase that to twice a week this year. Instead of formal exercise, I often do "power cleaning" once or twice a week; or what I call "power chores" around the house. For example, I may jog in place for a minute or so and then fold laundry. Then I may jog in place again for another minute and then put the laundry away! It's silly and it may not be something you want to do; but that is what I do! For me it is just easier to add some exercise intervals into my daily activities around the home than to set aside specific time for formal, planned physical exercise. On the days I do exercise formally with a walk or an aerobics video, I may eat up to 1800 or even 1900 calories on those days.

I usually eat about 5 times a day; each time about 300 calories. I eat this way not because I planned to eat this way. I eat this way because this is how my stomach-based hunger signals tell me how to eat. For many people this is their stomach-based hunger pattern too – but yours may be different. You need to eat the way your stomach signals you! Your signals may create a different eating pattern for you.

Also, your signals may vary from day to day depending on what you ate the day before or based on your level of physical activity. For example, you may be very hungry at breakfast time and you may actually need to eat a 700 calorie breakfast before your stomach feels better and the hunger signal dissipates. If this happens, you most likely won't get your next true stomach hunger signal until 6 or maybe even 7 hours later; meaning you may need to eat your next meal, typically lunch, later in the day than normal. Then at lunch, and dinner, you will likely find that you only need about 300-500 calories for each meal in order to satisfy your hunger signal. If you stay up late at night (as I do when I am writing) you may find that you have a hunger signal late at night. You can eat again then but be extra careful to only eat what you need to make the signal dissipate.

Overall, I think you will be very amazed at just how well your true, God given, stomach-based hunger signal regulates your need and desires to align with exactly what you need to do to be your best weight! By paying close attention to your true hunger signal, and eating when it signals "my stomach is near empty;" and stopping when it signals "my stomach feels better now;" **you will be amazed at just how natural it becomes to eat the exact amount of calories needed to lose weight and to reach your ideal weight!** Your body was created by the all-knowing, master-creator, God, to know and to signal to you exactly what it needs in the exact amount that it needs!

8.

Launching Further

I want to end this book with an encouragement. Use what you have learned in this book as a launching pad for helping others and helping yourself. Use the meditation strategy to help you in other areas of your life where you need to break free from specific temptations and habits in order to be closer to the Lord.

I also hope that the practice of Biblical meditation will be a beginning point for you. Biblical meditation is a simple and doable practice that I hope will become a starting point for you in growing closer to God's will for your life. As you practice Biblical meditation more and more over the first several weeks, you may find that you are becoming closer to the Lord and you may feel more comfortable and more encouraged to pray your own prayers in your own words. You may find that you want to dig deeper into reading the Bible. Both of these are fine actions to take in place of the recommended meditations.

First - this is my hope and prayer for you-- that these simple, effective meditations will help to focus and sustain you like they have sustained me through a difficult battle with my own weight and health. Next, I hope doing the meditations will bring you to a point of craving further closeness with God, so that you are fully comfortable with approaching Him more personally and intimately in your own prayers and Bible reading times.

Finally, I want to praise and thank the Lord God, our Father and Creator, for holding back on initially answering my prayers. I praise Him and thank Him for helping me to learn how Biblical meditation is such a simple and powerful tool for overcoming temptations and obstacles in life. Finally, I praise Him and thank Him for allowing me an opportunity to share what I have learned with others; so that my testimony may bring glory to Him and help to others. To Him be the glory, always.

About the Author

Sherry Elaine Evans has lived in the Houston, Texas metro-area for most of her life, and currently lives in the suburb of Spring, Texas. She is married with two daughters, both currently elementary school aged. Sherry holds a bachelor's degree in Psychology and English Literature from Baylor University and a master's degree in Educational Psychology from the University of Houston. Sherry is the author of several Christian Living books. She has a passion for knowing, teaching, and inspiring through the words and teachings of Christ. As she has grown older; Sherry has become more aware of the human need to rely on God's help, love, and guidance every single day, in big matters and in small. All we have to do is make time for Him and give Him a priority focus in our lives.

Other Works by Sherry Elaine Evans:

14 Days of Words with Jesus: How Do I Discover God's Will for Me?

14 Days of Parables with Jesus: Why Is There So Much Trouble in Life?

14 Days of Miracles with Jesus: How Do I See God Working Today?

21402655R00037

Made in the USA
San Bernardino, CA
19 May 2015